EVELYN M. FIELD

SOCIAL SMARTS HANDBOOK

Navigating Friendships
and Challenging People

SOCIAL SMARTS HANDBOOK

Navigating Friendships
and Challenging People

EVELYN M. FIELD

Published in 2025 by Amba Press, Melbourne, Australia
www.ambapress.com.au

© Evelyn Field 2025

All rights reserved. No part of this book may be reproduced or transmitted in any form or by any means, electronic or mechanical, including photocopying, recording or by any information storage and retrieval system, without prior permission in writing from the publisher.

Cover design: Tess McCabe
Internal design: Production Works
Editor: Rica Dearman

ISBN: 9781923215863 (pbk)
ISBN: 9781923215870 (ebk)

A catalogue record for this book is available from the National Library of Australia.

Disclaimer

This book is written for students as a simple guide. It cannot be used as a replacement for evidence-based therapy.

Please consult a registered and specialist psychologist for treatment.

Contents

Dedication		vi
Introduction: How animals are like us		1
Chapter 1	The range of social skills	7
Chapter 2	Why do we need social smarts?	15
Chapter 3	Manage your feelings	21
Chapter 4	Understand why others behave the way they do	29
Chapter 5	Improve your self-esteem	35
Chapter 6	Communication skills	43
Chapter 7	Manage difficult, dodgy or dangerous people	51
Chapter 8	Everyone needs a social support system	61
Conclusion		73
References		75

Dedication

For Miriam, from whom I learned the importance of social connection, and for every young person learning how to connect, belong and be themselves, you are not alone.

Years ago, I hoped to write a book about shyness and social being, because I realised how my family and friends make my life meaningful, but for three decades, life took me in another direction – researching and writing about bullying at school and work, a topic closely tied to our social smarts.

When Alicia Cohen invited me to write about social skills, the timing felt right. Thanks to what we now understand about animals, loneliness and brain injuries, it's more significant than ever to improve our social smarts – for our health, our happiness and even our survival.

Acknowledgement

I'm very grateful to Alicia Cohen, Rica Dearman and Alicia's team for enabling me to write the book I had envisioned more than 30 years ago, and thanks to Sean Doyle for his inspiring title.

Introduction: How animals are like us

Harry was my first animal coach. He was a small, adorable Papillon. He loved strawberries and had a funny way of tilting his head, grunting and asking for more. While he liked hiding during the day, he enjoyed cuddles from my clients. Harry wasn't afraid to chase birds, but he always ran to me for protection from the cleaner's noisy vacuum. When his big sister, Bufy, tried to boss him around, he'd stand firm, turn around and point his big bushy tail at her face.

Many animals sense your feelings and show empathy. I'm sure your pet stays close to you when you're upset and comforts you. Both animals and humans have similar ways of feeling emotions like happiness or sadness, anger and fear, because our brains have developed in similar ways. We both have chemicals in our brains called neurotransmitters, like dopamine and serotonin. Dopamine is linked to pleasure, and serotonin regulates feelings and helps us calm down.

Animals show how they feel through their behaviour, body language and sounds. A happy dog might wag its tail, while dolphins surf waves when they're excited. When animals feel pain, they might yelp, limp or protect the hurt part of their body. Like us, animals play with each other, show affection by cuddling or grooming, and even grieve when they lose someone significant.

Animals react in different ways when they confront danger. Rabbits hide to stay safe, while other animals attack; saltwater crocodiles trick their prey by hiding underwater to surprise them and yank them into a death roll. Certain animals, such as chimpanzees, dolphins and elephants, are known for their intelligence. They can solve problems, use tools and show emotions like joy or sadness. Like humans, some animals are outgoing and social, while others are quieter and keep to themselves. When you spend lots of time with animals, you recognise what their sounds and actions mean – whether they're playful, afraid or curious. These behaviours show how connected many animals are to each other – and to humans.

Family chat

- Discuss with your family how animals show their feelings, and why it's important for humans to understand them.

Social survival

Dunbar (2009) said that the social brain hypothesis proposes that primates, including humans, apes and monkeys, have bigger brains for body size compared to all other vertebrates, because they live in complex social groups. Their brains have grown bigger over time to help them understand relationships in these groups, and to work together and get along with others.

Although some animal behaviours are instinctive, like humans, most animals learn how to communicate, socialise and survive from their families. Primates, dolphins, elephants and magpies live in groups and have developed larger brains to recognise family, understand social rules, communicate and work together to survive.

Animals like leopards and tigers, which prefer to be alone, have smaller brains because they don't need as much brainpower for socialising, since they hunt and survive alone. This connection between social structure and brain size is often referred to as the 'social brain hypothesis', which proposes that the demands of social living drive the evolution of larger brains. No wonder lions struggle without their pride, and animals that trail behind their group are more vulnerable to attack!

Thus, our brains have grown to accommodate the hard work of building and managing enjoyable friendships and challenging relationships – something every teenager can relate to!

Journal jotting

- What social survival skills have you noticed with your pets or other animals on social media or at a zoo?
- How would you describe the connection between a pet and its owner?
- Can you remember a time when an animal understood your feelings? How did you feel?

Animals aren't robots – they feel and understand other animals and human beings by using their mirror neurons and different behaviours to communicate. When we take time to learn what they're communicating, we build a stronger connection. During the COVID-19 pandemic, psychologists doing therapy by videoconference often noticed how pets mirrored their owners' feelings. That's why some animals like dogs, horses and parrots are used in therapy for people dealing with stress, anxiety, trauma and depression.

Pets or other animals help you feel calmer, happier, more confident and less alone. Some people believe their pets are more understanding than their family members or friends! Some people choose pets that resemble them, such as similar hair colour, body shape or personalities, like shy or playful. This happens because we feel comfortable with pets that remind us of ourselves.

> ### Pair and share
> ♦ Swap with a friend some photos of owners who look like their pets – make sure you get their permission first.

What does this all mean?

When I meet students who feel shy, lonely or are having a tough time socially, I sometimes suggest simple ways they can improve their social skills. Many say, *"That's not me"* or *"I can't do that"*. Then I remind them, *"If an animal with a smaller brain than you can do this, so can you!"* Everyone can improve their communication skills by listening, asking for help and learning from feedback, and no type of psychological 'label' should stop them from improving their social skills.

Although human beings have a more highly developed brain than animals, there are lots of behaviours and skills that we have in common. That's why I say, if a little dog like Harry can learn how to communicate and behave in different ways, so can most human beings, whose brains are far larger, more complex and more evolved. Thus, I hope to prove my point with animal examples throughout this book, and hopefully, I can convince you that if an animal has learnt a social skill, then so can you!

This book will help you learn the skills you need to develop simple, successful, social survival skills, using the analogies from animals along the way.

Superpowers

A **superpower** is a skill you practise until it works very well. Dogs have amazing superpowers. They have learnt how to use eye contact, head tilts and paws to score treats, walkies and belly rubs. Although some kids are born more sociable, anyone can learn. Practice turns a small skill into a social superpower. I've got a few throughout this book – you can collect yours, too. Write them down as you read through the book.

Reflection questions

Throughout this book, you will come across questions/exercises in boxes that have been broken down into different themes – you will have already come across three of them in this introduction. Here is a list of all of the themes in this book:

1. **Journal jotting** – these include questions for you to think about and note in your journal.
2. **Check it out** – although it's easy to get advice from others or treat all information like a computer-generated AI request, you also need to create your own truth.
3. **Take action** – when you know what to do, don't hesitate; just follow the instructions.
4. **Family chat** – discuss these issues with your family to compare their expectations with your own.
5. **Pair and share** – discuss this with a friend to help clarify your thoughts.
6. **Just do it** – you may not know exactly what to do, but have a go anyway, as later constructive feedback will help you.
7. **Let it go** – nobody's perfect, and some things aren't worth worrying about.
8. **Give it a go** – it's OK to take a chance and try something new, as long as it's not bad. Then review the outcome.

Conducting these exercises will help you build social skills to make your friendships more meaningful and enjoyable.

Note: This book is designed to educate parents as well as their kids!

CHAPTER 1

The range of social skills

The Galápagos Islands are home to different sea and land animals. Most animals feel safe there because they lack predators. They appear relaxed and sociable, not shy or aggressive; they don't usually fight or squawk over territory, mates or food, and back off when necessary. Although most sharks are territorial, the Galápagos Islands sharks are not usually dangerous or hostile. However, the iguanas look identical but differ. Shy iguanas hide in hilly areas to avoid threats, whereas sociable iguanas lie around the beach, sprawled over different species like siblings or mates.

Human beings are social beings

Around the world, people grow up with different traditions, customs and values which influence how they interact socially. Humans are basically social beings; we need to connect to others to survive. Even in your school, you might notice classmates acting, talking or dressing in ways influenced by their family culture. I'm sure that you're also different, more like a patchwork doll.

Some kids are reserved, others are sociable. Most Australians are friendly, relaxed and easy to talk to. Their relationships are open, fair and focused on enjoying time together without too many rules. In contrast, many Asian cultures focus on showing respect and avoiding embarrassment for themselves, their families and their social group.

In countries like Korea, politeness and respect are essential, while Japanese students follow cultural values that emphasise hierarchy, being humble and blending in.

People communicate in many different ways. Some cultures use lots of gestures and body language, while others prefer clear, direct speech. In some places, touch is an important part of connection, while in others, it's forbidden.

By understanding and respecting these differences, we can build better friendships with people from all backgrounds. Learning about someone's culture shows understanding and helps us connect. Remember, your social skills can change depending on who you're with, where you are and what else is happening. Everyone can learn to connect socially and suitably in their own way.

Family chat

- Why is it important to understand and respect how people from different cultures or backgrounds behave and communicate? Share examples.

Social skills

Children need to learn basic social skills from their family, like expressing courtesy and respect, caring and collaborating, and respecting the thoughts and feelings of others. Your family demonstrates how to interact with different types of people, including those who are challenging. Some families empower their children, while some squash their children by expecting them to obey their rules.

Later on, as a teenager, you will learn different social skills from your friends and classmates. You will learn how to collaborate with others, solve problems together and interact with a variety of people. Both your home and school play important roles in helping you develop and refine your social skills.

Shyness and other social challenges

Shyness affects how you feel about yourself, make friends, manage tricky social situations and chase your personal and career goals when you're older. Shy kids struggle to enter a room, make eye contact, smile or start conversations because they fear feeling foolish, embarrassed or rejected. Beginning new social connections is hard for shy kids.

Shyness is connected to brain areas that handle stress, like the amygdala and hippocampus, so shy kids have higher levels of stress hormones, like cortisol. The late psychologist Philip Zimbardo said shyness comes from a mixture of things, like your family, genes, culture and how you cope with challenges.

While you're young, your family is your social skills role model; later on, your shyness will decrease as you develop better social skills or disguise them. Some kids become more confident when they socialise outside school and when they're older. You can improve your social skills with practice, even if you have 'problems' or fit somewhere on a 'spectrum'. As a psychologist, I've seen many shy students make friends within a few months by using simple strategies like those I've included in this book.

> ### Give it a go
>
> ♦ Discuss with a friend any social situations where you feel less shy and why you think this is.
>
> ♦ Find a chat group where you can discover what others do to feel less shy.
>
> ♦ Research: find famous people who were shy.

Social anxiety

Social anxiety disorder (SAD), also known as social phobia, occurs when you feel petrified about being seen and judged by others. Your fear makes it hard to connect with other people. It can happen at any time in your life, due to trauma, past experiences or personal traits. The good news is that it's common and can be treated.

> ### Journal jotting
>
> ♦ What are some situations where you feel tense about being judged? Why do you think this is?
>
> ♦ What could you do to feel more confident?

Neuro labels

Mental health professionals like labels that change every decade or so. Currently, we divide people into two types:

- **Neurotypical:** The child's social brain understands and responds to most situations in ways that most people consider normal.
- **Neurodiverse:** This child's brain works differently, like those with autism, ADHD, dyslexia or Tourette syndrome, or following severe trauma.

Everyone has their own unique way of experiencing the world – even geniuses think differently! There's not one way of becoming a 'normal' social being – everyone belongs somewhere on the long continuum of social skills.

Schools should accept neurodiverse students as being different and incorporate their unique strengths into the school community, with specially designed programs where appropriate. Even neurodiverse students can learn simple social skills.

Family chat

- Sit down with your family and get some ideas as to how you can become socially more included at school, regardless of how your brain functions.

(Here's a tip: ask them to video you for a few minutes and then play it back, with or without feedback. Repeat this a few times until you know what to do.)

The impact of the COVID-19 pandemic (2020+)

"In 2020, teens spent 70% less time with friends than in 2003; 40% of teens in 21 countries often feel lonely" (UNICEF, 2021).

During the coronavirus pandemic, fish in aquariums and zoo animals became lonely without visitors, while many students' social lives changed. With schools closed, kids spent more time at home, had less face-to-face time with friends, but connected through social media, phone calls and virtual events. Many were lonely and missed out on a physical connection with their friends or making new ones. Others were more fortunate and focused on closer friends, driveway dates, bike rides, footy at the local park and neighbours.

The pandemic affected everyone differently, depending on their age, personality and social support. Some students became more shy, anxious or depressed because it was harder to socialise, and very challenging to return to school and resume a normal social life. Whereas, for others, life returned to normal. The pandemic reminded us that we are social beings who need to connect with others in different ways to feel better about ourselves.

Social media

Social media is a great tool for staying in touch with friends and family, especially when you can't see them in person. It's fast, easy and helpful for sharing information and connecting. But while social media helps with communication, it can't replace the real thing.

Being with others in person, sharing experiences, reading their body language, smelling their scent or noting their body movements helps you build stronger, authentic relationships. Relying too much on social media makes you feel more isolated, stressed and depressed. Sadly, online, people can hide who they are, making it easier for others to get conned, scammed or bullied, thus making it harder to trust others.

Pair and share

♦ Find a friend to discuss whether or not the pandemic changed the way you connect with other students and what differences there are between online and in-person interactions.

Social being

"Recently, fMRI scans have demonstrated how the teenager's brain changes over the course of their adolescent years" (Blakemore & Mills, 2014).

From the days when people lived in tribes or villages to the social lives we have today, you could survive without friends or social connections, although it reduces your life expectancy, and it's far harder to deal with stress or tough times on your own. Having strong social connections, like friends, family or a supportive community, helps you feel included, supported, happier and physically healthier.

Social support makes it easier to handle difficult situations because you're not facing them alone and you can always obtain useful feedback. Social support reduces your stress, protects your mind and body, and helps you stay healthier while coping with life's challenges.

Being sociable and connecting with others is an important part of life; it's key to becoming resilient (which means bouncing back from challenges). Whereas, feeling lonely for a long time causes stress, depression and sadness, which is why loneliness is becoming a serious health hazard.

Family chat

- Why is having close friends or family important for your physical, emotional and social wellbeing?
- Why does seeking help from friends or family make it easier to bounce back from stressful situations?
- Does your family cope well with challenges, and if not, what else could they do?

CHAPTER 2

Why do we need social smarts?

Soobin was a young dolphin who loved exploring but felt lonely. One day, she saw a group of dolphins playing with a shiny seashell and timidly swam over to say hello. At first, the dolphins were surprised, but soon they clicked back, inviting her to join. As they played, Soobin learned how the group worked together, listening to clicks and whistles to keep the game going. She realised dolphins helped each other find food and stay safe. Soobin felt happy being part of the pod and knew everyone needs friends to thrive.

What's the problem?

Some teens grow up in close communities with family and neighbours nearby. While they may lack privacy, they have lots of local kids to befriend, which helps them feel safe and socially included. Other teens lack this kind of support – some move homes frequently, lack extended family or close neighbours. This makes it harder to develop social skills and handle tough situations. Sadly, while our brain is wired to socialise in person, many teens are spending more time alone, due to the increase of smartphones and the pandemic.

Isolation and loneliness

"When researchers isolated male mice for two weeks, they noticed that the mice could no longer activate their medial prefrontal cortex [which means they could no longer turn on the brain cells in the part of the brain that helps them to understand and think about others] neurons and couldn't socialise again" (Lim et al., 2020).

Most kids feel lonely at times, even when people are close by. Some find socialising hard because they feel uncomfortable creating close social connections or are fearful of being bullied. However, staying lonely for too long can harm your health and shorten your life. Loneliness changes parts of your brain, such as your prefrontal cortex and amygdala, making it harder to deal with stress, anxiety and schoolwork. It harms your body by raising blood pressure and weakening your immune system. Whether it's feeling excluded by friends or unsupported by family, loneliness seriously affects your mind and body.

> ### Check it out
> ♦ Do your research – what's the difference between being alone and being lonely?

The social brain

My sister had two tawny owls in her big garden. When she moved to a new apartment, the owls followed! When her grandson stayed with her for two weeks, the owls disappeared. Even though they only saw her through a window, they knew when her grandson had gone, as the owls then returned, bringing their baby. Once, when my sister bobbed her head, the baby mirrored her!

Social neuroscience is the study of how our brains helps us to connect with others, including how we make friends and how we handle social situations. The social brain hypothesis, defined on page 3, claims that human beings are naturally wired to connect with others and that these connections are essential for our wellbeing. This means that your brain has special parts that help you understand social behaviours – what others think and feel, what you're doing, who you're with and how you're interacting. This helps you build shared social or working relationships, which is beneficial to teamwork and group projects. And when we feel lonely, our brain reacts in the same way that it does when we feel physical pain – this shows just how much we need social bonds, to feel healthy and safe.

Different parts of your brain create social connections to help identify your own reactions, notice what others are doing or feeling, and even copy them. These brain networks track your good and bad social experiences by learning from the feedback you receive. Building social connections and spending time with friends is important for maintaining your physical and emotional wellbeing. While social media helps you stay connected, real-life friendships are key to feeling happy and supported.

Social sections in your brain

Did you know that your brain has at least 10 special sections that work together to help you understand people, make friends and stay safe in groups? Your brain is built for social connections – it is a superlative social computer! Here's how some of its parts help you:

- **Prefrontal Cortex (PFC)**
  This part of your brain sits right behind your forehead. It helps you understand how other people think and feel; it helps you make future plans; and it controls your actions to make clever choices in different situations.

- **Amygdala**
  This tiny, almond-shaped part sits deep inside your brain. It helps you feel and understand emotions like fear, anger and excitement. It helps you spot when someone else is upset, so you can respond appropriately.

- **Temporal parietal junction (TPJ)**
  This part helps you guess what other people might be thinking or feeling, like mind-reading! It helps you figure out why people act the way they do.

- **Anterior cingulate cortex (ACC)**
  This part helps you deal with your own emotions and feel empathy, which includes caring about how others feel. It helps you handle emotional and physical pain.

- **Fusiform face area (FFA)**
  This area helps you recognise faces and read people's expressions, so you can identify who they are and how they're feeling.

- **Hippocampus**
  This part stores your memories, especially important social moments, like fun times with friends or lessons you've learned from talking to others.

- **Nucleus accumbens**
  This is your 'reward centre'. It makes you feel happy and excited when something good happens, like making a new friend or reaching a goal. It keeps you motivated to achieve.

- **Hypothalamus**
  This small but powerful section controls your basic needs – like eating, sleeping and de-stressing. It helps release chemicals, like oxytocin, which help you trust and bond with others.

- **Superior temporal sulcus (STS)**
  This part helps you read clues from people's faces, bodies and eyes to understand what they are feeling and thinking. It helps you 'read the room', so you know how to act.

- **Mirror neurons**
  These special brain cells help you understand what others are doing and feeling. When you see someone smile, frown or yawn, your mirror neurons light up – it is like your brain is copying them! This helps you feel connected to others and shows empathy. They are a social **superpower**.

Just do it

- You can strengthen your mirror neurons by listening carefully, paying attention to people's actions and trying to see things from their point of view. When you practise this, you become better at making friends, working in teams and helping others feel safe and understood. The more you use these parts of your brain, the better you become at connecting, cooperating and caring for others – and that's what makes humans strong social beings.

Resilience – what's that?

Resilience means bouncing back from tough times and handling challenges while still appreciating your life. It's about thinking positively, managing your feelings and asking others for help when required. Throughout history, people have worked together in groups like families, tribes and villages because it's extremely difficult to deal with problems alone without damaging yourself. Research shows that we need friends, family and communities to support us, especially when life is tough. Besides, we achieve more with support and constructive feedback.

Pair and share

♦ Resilient teens mess up, ask for back-up, laugh it off and bounce back like champs when life gets tough. Sit down with a friend and share some examples of when you were both being resilient.

CHAPTER 3

Manage your feelings

Capybaras are the world's biggest rodents and are native to South America. They're calm, gentle and love living in groups. People call them 'nature's chill animals' because they stay calm and feel safe living in their groups which protect them. They enjoy water, eating plants and relaxing, making them great friends to other animals.

The survival instinct

All living things, including humans, have a basic survival instinct to protect themselves when they feel that their life is being threatened. When something causes us distress, our brain releases specific hormones to take action and manage these feelings to survive. This is OK in moderation, but what happens if you can't manage excessive feelings appropriately? Although your feelings are designed to protect you from further harm, they can make the situation worse. We all know someone who keeps everything inside but implodes, pushing kind people away, while others broadcast their distress and then explode – neither is good for a person's health.

"We intuitively believe social and physical pain are radically different kinds of experiences, yet the way our brains treat them suggests that they are more similar than we imagine" (Lieberman, 2013).

Therefore, it's important to discover how anxiety and anger affect your brain and to find better ways of managing them so that your brain and body aren't further injured by toxic levels of these powerful hormones. Thus, while a moderate amount of stress motivates you to work and succeed, too much stress sabotages everything you say or do and undermines your social connections.

So, a basic task in building your social networks is to regulate your feelings so that they don't interfere with your friendships. This involves identifying your feelings, quantifying them to see how mild or severe they are, and taking action to release or reduce intense feelings. You will find that students who are easy-going and relaxed find it easier to meet and greet, connect and create stronger friendships.

Here's how it works

1. Something bad happens, like not finishing homework, or running out of your favourite snack. You become stressed or angry, which triggers parts of your brain.

2. Your hypothalamus identifies this stress and sends a message to your pituitary gland (also in your brain).

3. Your pituitary gland tells your adrenal glands (which sit above your kidneys) to release specific stress hormones.

4. The adrenal glands release cortisol and adrenaline (and other hormones). These hormones activate your body to take action and react to the threatening event.

5. These hormones quickly spread through your whole body, energising you to confront the danger. This is your '**fight, flight or freeze**' instinct.

6. While your body follows its survival instinct, its primitive reaction to stress alters your brain, body, appearance, health, relationships, concentration and so on, sometimes forever.

7. As a social being, you need to reprogram your instinctual stressful feelings to be regulated by your prefrontal cortex. In other words, once you're aware of your stressors, find better ways of managing them to reduce harm to your brain, body and relationships.

What does this mean?

Your voice and body language, like a nod or a look, display your feelings and alter your relationships. If you look grumpy or angry, you may appear threatening, attract the wrong crowd or invite further attack. If you're very stressed, friendships become more difficult as you lack energy to engage and empathise. Besides, no one feels comfortable around a worrywart. Some kids do nothing, so their friends move away.

Adolescence is a difficult time for managing feelings, as your hormones fluctuate. However, just like a pet can sense your feelings, your friends can sense when you're upset. This is the time to share a small sample of what you're feeling so they understand, don't take your moods personally or feel rejected. Being physically healthy – through good sleep, eating well and exercising – also improves your mood and social life. When you're calm and confident, people will chill out around you and want to spend time with you.

Take action

- You can handle tricky feelings by using the smart part of your brain, your prefrontal cortex. This helps you stay calm, think clearly and talk to others in a way that solves problems instead of creating them. Instead of automatically using your fight, flight or freeze instinct, why don't you find better F words to manage your stresses, like feisty, flexible or friendly?

Just do it

- How would you feel if you regulated your feelings of anxiety and anger more effectively?
- Would it help to explore other methods of release?
- What else can you do to improve your diet, exercise, sleep and mindful behaviours?

Here's the formula

A. Identify

Whether you're hot or cold, hungry or thirsty, you'll guess what action to take anytime. On a hot day, you'll drink more often; if it's a cold day, like a cat or dog, you'll find the warmest place to sit or wear warmer clothing. Likewise, if you're feeling angry or scared, it builds up. If you don't release those toxic feelings, you'll either bottle or burst – or both. It's not surprising that when you're extremely stressed, your instinctive mind-body networks can make you physically sick.

Like our basic colours of red, yellow, blue and black and white, you need to identify your four major feelings, which include your anger, fear, sadness and joy. To express it more simply, 'Are you feeling sad, mad, bad or glad, or a combination of these feelings?' In this handbook, I will focus on your anger and fear, which form an essential part of your basic survival instinct. They can help keep you safe when you're in danger and motivate you to take action.

Check it out

- Name some stressful feelings you've experienced today.
- Did you notice them in different parts of your body? For example, did you clench your hands or scratch yourself?
- Did you do something annoying as a consequence? For example, when angry, did you break a glass or stub your toe, scream or throw stuff around – even if it hurts other people?

B. Quantify

Although a few pieces of very dark chocolate are healthy, eating the whole packet at once isn't. It's the same when you're hungry; you decide whether to have a bite-size, snack-size or man-size portion. Likewise, it's sensible to assess how much your feelings are affecting you. Imagine a 10-point scale. If you're feeling a little angry, like 3/10, you can release this minor worry later (like delaying a meal when you're moderately hungry); if you're feeling 6/10 angry, then take action to lower it, as it can affect your behaviours; but if you're a 9.5/10, then act immediately, otherwise it will impact upon everything you do, leading to mistakes, accidents and also hurting someone's feelings.

Although it's not always practical to release your feelings, sometimes naming and quantifying is a beginning. Then you may say, *"I'm 8/10 angry. I can't scream in class, but I can imagine doing it now, or I'll hit a ball after school."*

Check it out

♦ When have you experienced a little anger or fear, a moderate amount or a severe amount?

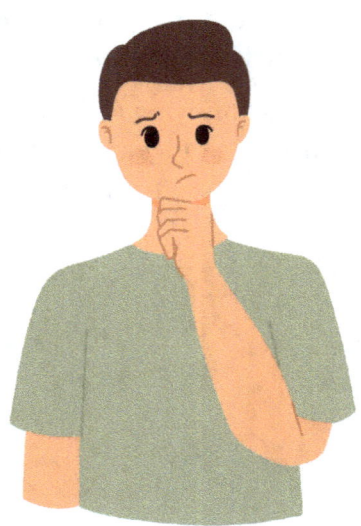

C. Release

By now, you've discovered that when you feel bad, it can injure parts of your brain and body. When you drink too much, you visit the bathroom more often; likewise, when you're very stressed, you need to release your emotional pain. If you don't release painful feelings, they may harm your body. When you study or exercise, a timetable is the best plan for developing the skills you need. Thus, if you're very stressed, plan your timetable to release three to five times a day. If you're moderately stressed, release once a day, and if you're hardly stressed, once a week may do. For example, if you're a little angry, yell at the footy once a week, or exercise several times a week, but if you're extremely angry, then release a few times a day.

There are many different ways to release painful feelings, so make a list of around three to five options that you can use at school or home. Check out anything that reduces your anxiety, anger and pain (refer to *Bully Blocking*, 2023). Avoid medication, but Rescue Remedy helps with stress and Panadol may work for social rejection.

Here are some release options:

Verbal: sing, shout, whistle, verbalise, for example, *"I feel"*

Physical: deep breathing, running, punching, dancing, hitting, kicking

Biochemical: comfort food or drink (in moderation)

Olfactory: incense, scents, open fire

Visual: photos, special objects, nature walks

Auditory: waves, music, drumming

Mindfulness: music, games, apps, reading, social media (in moderation)

Placebo: anything that helps but doesn't hurt you or anyone else

Family chat

- What can you and your family do to release painful feelings so that everyone feels better?

Use your mirror neurons

When your mirror neurons are working, you gain support and empathy from others. You know that you're not alone and that other people understand and help where possible. Verbal and written messages of support are helpful and healing.

Check it out

- Find three examples of how your mirror neurons worked well.
- How could you improve some of your social relationships?
- What happens if you remarked to a friend who's not listening, *"Is there something wrong with your mirror neurons today?"*
- How can you expand your mirror neurons to show empathy for another student's lived experience?

CHAPTER 4

Understand why others behave the way they do

"Parrots that were abandoned and traumatised bond better with patients with similar challenges. For example, a parrot with a broken wing connected with a veteran with a crooked elbow, while a parrot with epilepsy chose a veteran with seizures! This shows that sharing similar struggles can help us understand and support each other" (Siebert, 2016).

There are always reasons why people behave the way they do. Instead of blaming yourself or others, try to understand what's behind the behaviour. Start by understanding your own feelings and actions, like your background, personal attributes, current stresses, handicaps or past experiences, and then try to understand others. This will help you become more compassionate and create better friendships; it's another social **superpower**.

Understand yourself and others

While it's essential to treat everyone with respect and kindness, understanding what makes each person unique, including yourself, helps everyone build better social connections. Our unique personality is shaped by several factors:

- **Genetics:** These influence our hair colour, height, intelligence, talents, personality, and physical and mental health.

Family chat
- What genetic factors like being extremely tall or on a spectrum affect you?

- **Family position:** Families are like teams, where everyone has their own role and experiences. If you're the oldest child, you are expected to become a good role model and follow your parents' instructions. Middle children have more freedom and good social skills but may feel overlooked. The youngest child gets more attention but is treated differently. If you're an only child, having lots of attention is nice, but it's lonely without siblings. Every role is different, but that makes every family unique.

Pair and share
- Discuss with a classmate what it's like to occupy a designated position in your family, and what's it like if you're in a blended family.

♦ **Family and cultural background:** Your family, friends, cultural or religious environment play a significant role in influencing who you are, as do major stresses like moving overseas, the death of a loved one and family sickness.

Check it out

- A family genogram is a map that shows who's who in your family and significant things about them. Look up examples on the internet and then draw your family genogram. Write down a brief personal description of each member. You can ask your parents for help.

- Try to include grandparents and great-grandparents to learn more about your family's history. It can show where your family came from, their culture and religion, places they've lived and big events in their lives. Write down what their social life was like at your age and whether they're more or less sociable now.

Journal jotting

- Life events and experiences shape who you are, so reflect on what you've learned about yourself and how your family background has impacted the way you think, feel and behave.

Different faces from faraway places

Kids can be very different in appearance, cultural background and social experiences at your school. Students from other cultures may relate differently to their classmates, especially if they migrate in their teens. However, as most of us live in a multicultural society, it's important to understand their backgrounds to connect and become inclusive, where possible. It helps to be more aware of differences, for example, most Asian kids focus first on reading the room, while most Aussie kids try to dominate it!

Family chat

♦ Share some of the different social customs and behaviours that some students have at your school or in your neighbourhood.

Understand change

Charles Darwin discovered that finches adapted to their environment in the Galápagos Islands. Likewise, we also need to learn how to adapt to the constant changes around us. The COVID-19 pandemic showed us that change happens for everyone. Whether it's in our neighbourhoods, technology or the climate, things are always changing. As we grow, our bodies, thoughts and feelings change, too. Learning to adjust to these changes is a normal and important part of life. Adapting helps us stay strong and keep up with the world around us.

Journal jotting

♦ Can you name three to five things that have stayed the same in your life and three to five things that have changed in the past year? (This could be technology, health, moving, growing up or losing someone.) Have these changes affected you? If so, how?

How can you understand others better?

Just like an animal checks you out before moving closer or away, try to understand the people you meet. Pay attention to how they appear – friendly or unfriendly, safe or unsafe, stable or unpredictable. However, consider the challenges they may be facing at school or at home. You need to listen carefully (without constantly interrupting), ask respectful questions and absorb their feedback. I'm sure you have more things in common than you imagined and can appreciate why they behave in certain ways. This helps you see life from their perspective. Understanding someone else's life helps you build stronger connections, or you can move away politely.

Pair and share

- Find a friend, look closely and guess what their life is like at school or at home. Then, ask them if you were totally correct, partly correct or mistaken.

- Change places and repeat. How well did you both guess what each other's life was like?

CHAPTER 5

Improve your self-esteem

Bufy was a feisty, friendly little dog who loved playing, enjoyed belly rubs and eating. When she felt threatened, she acted tough, even with cows. She growled when she felt scared or angry, her fur stood up and her tail became upright. When she did something wrong, she tucked her tail under, lowered her head and tried to sneak away. She knew who she was.

Have you noticed how some kids are liked by nearly everyone? They're confident, friendly and respectful, creating a positive energy wherever they go. They don't gossip or obsess over minor problems. They treat others kindly, provided they reciprocate. They enjoy connecting with all kinds of people but maintain clear boundaries. Their positive self-esteem enables others to feel good being around them. Thus, being cheerful and optimistic is another social **superpower**.

Although your self-esteem fluctuates according to what's happening in your life, it's like a mirror reflecting how you appreciate yourself, as you are right now. Your self-esteem influences how you speak, behave and connect with others. It grows from your experiences with family, friends, your abilities and coping with your ups and downs. If these are constructive, your self-esteem will be positive and assertive, but if you experience major stresses during childhood, you may focus on your flaws and failures. Then you lose confidence and faith in yourself or others and become overly critical or distrustful. Sadly, over time, severe stress changes your body at a cellular level, making it harder to manage social challenges and build good relationships. Thus, building your self-esteem and becoming assertive is another social **superpower** that helps you connect positively with others.

Adolescence

As you move from childhood into adolescence, your body, mind and emotions change. So, while you refuse to wear what your mum buys, you dress like everyone else. Being a teenager can be tough, no matter how good you look, how smart you are or how many friends you think you have or don't have. Your mind and body are maturing, while schoolwork becomes more serious, preparing you for your future.

Meanwhile, your family, peers and the world can experience change at any stage. These changes affect your self-esteem.

Some of your stresses include:

- Physical appearance – *"Do I look OK?" "Am I attractive?"*
- Intellectual abilities – *"Am I below, average or above average with schoolwork?"*
- Emotional state – *"Do my feelings fluctuate or am I stable?"*
- Social status – *"Do I have good friends?" "Where do I belong?"*
- Managing expectations – *"How do I please myself and my family?"*
- Dealing with high-maintenance kids – *"How do I handle them?"*
- Finding a mentor – *"Who else can I discuss this with, apart from my parents?"*

Two major tasks of adolescence

Who am I?

It's important to know who you are at any given moment, which helps others understand you better. Like cleaning a foggy mirror, you boost your self-esteem by respecting your strengths and weaknesses, celebrating your successes, using feedback to learn from your mistakes and achieve more than you can alone and by accepting that nobody's perfect – not even you! Where possible, make constructive changes while accepting those areas that you can't change. However, the more you practice, the better you'll feel about yourself, and enjoy making real friends.

How do I belong?

Humans need social groups to survive because, without them, life is much harder. In school, it's important to develop social skills and build supportive friendships while still being yourself. Your role in a group can change depending on what others expect, but don't feel pressured to behave in ways you're not comfortable with. Some groups are friendly; some are threatened or jealous; others just exclude or bully, which boomerangs back later!

Five tips for improving self-esteem

1. Accept your mistakes

When you roll dice, you obtain different combinations of numbers. Throwing a 6 means *success*, while a 1 signifies a *learning experience*. If you roll the dice many times, you get more *successes* and more *learning experiences*. With practice, you can improve your self-esteem and social skills. But you'll never be perfect, because nobody is – unless they lie or cheat with loaded dice!

Adolescence is hard, but it's part of growing up. Changing your perspective can make things easier. Don't feel bad for flunking tricky or slippery goals. When you have a problem, don't blame yourself, but consider it from a different angle. The clue is to accept yourself as you are right now, including the mistakes you make, and apologise when appropriate. Be kind to yourself, then others will respect you more.

> ### Let it go
>
> ♦ Can you reframe your self-criticisms? For example, *"I hate my figure, but diet and exercise would help"*; *"I'm awful at maths, but I'll find a coach"*; *"I'm no good at that, but I tried"*; *"I'm not popular, but I have good friends"*.

2. Show gratitude

Gratitude means noticing and enjoying things that make you feel good, like ice cream, chocolate, nice weather or when someone shares their snacks, invites you to play or says something kind. When you feel grateful, your brain lights up and releases feel-good chemicals like dopamine and serotonin, which help you feel happy and calm. Gratitude also helps your prefrontal cortex (which helps you make good choices) and your hypothalamus (which helps your body stay balanced) work better. Practising gratitude improves your mental health, strengthens your friendships and even boosts your physical wellbeing.

Journal jotting

- Keep a Gratitude Diary and record at least three gratitudes a day. How does this affect your mood after a week, and after four weeks?

3. Give to yourself

Sometimes, parents, friends and teachers are too busy to give you self-esteem boosters, so you need to build your own self-esteem. Thus, being kind to yourself, especially when things are tough, is important, like doing things you enjoy and that aren't harmful. However, like learning a sport or playing an instrument, building self-esteem takes work, and you need to invest every day. This is another social **superpower** – when you accept yourself as you are right now, others can respect you and want to be with you.

Just do it

- What are three things that you can do regularly to feel better at home or at school?

Check it out

- Interview three adults to see how their self-esteem changed over the years. Were there some crucial or defining moments that altered their self-esteem, for example, finding a satisfying career, buying their first home, finding a partner, becoming a parent, failing exams or being involved in a severe car accident?

4. Give to others

When you're being kind, your brain releases chemicals like dopamine, serotonin and oxytocin. They boost your mood, reduce stress and help you feel more connected to others. Kindness strengthens your ability to understand and relate to others' feelings, making it easier to make friends and feel less lonely. Kind people tend to be healthier, more confident and well-liked. Even small acts, like smiling, chatting, helping someone or sharing potato chips, make a big difference and you can encourage others to be kind, too.

Check it out

- What have you done recently for a friend or family member, like helping them or making them smile?
- What could you do for someone else which you know will give them pleasure?

5. Allow others to give to you

Even though pop stars and sporting heroes rely on their coaches, many students believe it's possible to succeed alone. But collaborating with others can be far more empowering than struggling on your own. Thus, listening to others, accepting their help and saying *"thank you"* doesn't make you cowardly – their feedback will guarantee greater success for you. Besides, it's less stressful to obtain help sooner from others than to obsess about your stupid mistakes later.

When you let others help, everyone feels included and respected, allowing friendships to grow. Sharing your worries with friends means they can understand and support you. And if you need alone time, it's good to be honest and kind, like saying, *"I need some time alone"* or *"Maybe I'll join later"*. Ignoring people who are being nice to you can hurt their feelings, and they'll stop being friendly. Being kind, even when you need space, creates better friendships where everyone feels valued.

Journal jotting

- Write down some self-esteem boosters that you received from others but forgot to appreciate.

Pair and share feedback

- In a small group, Teenager A writes down three to five nice things about themselves.
- Teenager B writes three to five good things about Teenager A.
- Swap roles so each one gets a turn.
- Finally, share the compliments – did positive feedback change the way you feel about yourself?

CHAPTER 6

Communication skills

Wild parrots fly in pairs in close social groups, and each one has a unique identifying call, much like a human name. Early on, they learn to 'chat' so that they can communicate better with their own flock and other flocks. That's why they're so good at mimicking humans.

Many animals survive by following a leader and collaborating with their family. They rely on them to find food, care for their young and watch out for danger. They use different signals and behaviours to communicate and connect. They send visual signals by displaying their feathers, wagging their tails or changing their posture. They use sounds, like when they sing, howl, hiss or purr and touch, such as grooming, kicking or changing how close they stand to others.

Communication helps us get along with others, so it's important to be aware of how we behave and how others see us. Our family, culture and local community influence how we communicate, which changes in different situations. What works with your family might not work with friends. Therefore, paying attention to how you talk or swear, use acronyms, smile, make eye contact or use body language is essential. Asking questions and listening carefully shows you care.

Today, we have many ways to talk to each other, like texting, using social media or phoning. Talking face-to-face is best, but not always possible. Since the COVID-19 pandemic, some people feel nervous about making a phone call and prefer to text. But texting can lead to misunderstandings because it's hard to know what the other person really means, which makes it harder to feel connected.

> **Family chat**
>
> ♦ Introduce a new friend to your parents, and include special items of interest about them, for example, *"This is my friend Min-Ho; he's from Korea and loves ramen and kimchi."*

Non-verbal communication

People have always used clothes, jewellery, hairstyles and body language to show who they are and where they belong socially. In the past, fans conveyed special messages, whereas today, kids gesticulate with their phones or twiddle their hair. The way we greet others, like shaking hands or bowing, reflects our culture. It's much easier to fit in when we dress or act like our friends. No wonder most students adjust their school uniforms to follow current fashion fads. Therefore, paying attention to body language and respecting cultural differences helps everyone get along better.

> **Check it out**
>
> ♦ How can you be fashionable without buying expensive labels?

Some signs of non-verbal communication

Breathing: When you're stressed, your breathing becomes fast and shallow, which can threaten others, and they feel uncomfortable. When you breathe slowly and deeply, you become calm and confident, making it easier for others to relax around you.

Eyes: Eye contact shows you're engaged, listening and building connections, but in some cultures, it's disrespectful. In Western cultures, brief eye contact makes you appear genuine, smarter and trustworthy. If eye contact is inappropriate, show interest by facing the person, nodding and asking questions.

Smile: Smiling doesn't always mean that you're happy; it could be an invitation to connect, especially in Western cultures, and build trust. In Japan, smiling hides feelings, while in Russia it fosters suspicion. Australians smile more than many other cultures. Beware that we smirk when we feel uncomfortable, embarrassed, threatened, defensive or mask our aggression.

Face: Your face can show different expressions, which helps others understand what you're thinking and feeling. Thus, smiling or frowning appropriately makes your words more meaningful. Likewise, try to grasp what others expose on their face, and if you can't understand, then ask them. Thus, your facial muscles are a social **superpower** that enables you to show interest, concern or friendliness when appropriate.

***Did you know:** Domestic cats make 15 facial expressions, domestic horses make 17 facial expressions, dogs make 20+ facial expressions, while humans use 43 facial muscles to smile!*

Family chat
- Why are facial expressions important for making friends?

> ### Just do it
> - Try smiling at three to five people every day. What do you think will happen? Record it in your diary.

Body language: Body movements are crucial for communication and connection. They convey different messages and vary across cultures. For example, fidgeting can signal anxiety, while a calm posture reflects confidence and trustworthiness. Mirroring your body language and voice to that of others improves social connections.

Gestures: Have you ever had an older person pinch your cheeks to show they liked you? Most kids hate that! A pat on the shoulder or a kind word works better. Actions like patting or smiling are called *gestures* – movements that show our feelings. But gestures mean different things in different places; for example, a thumbs-up means 'good job' in some places, but is considered rude in others. It's helpful to know what gestures mean in different cultures, especially if you have friends from other cultures or plan to travel someday.

> ### Family chat
> - Are there any gestures that you, your friends or your family use that feel good or mean? If so, how could everyone encourage kinder ones and discourage the meaner ones?

Physical touch: Different kinds of physical contact give us different emotions. Friendly touches, like high-fives, pats on the back, hugs or holding hands, make us feel happy, safe and connected. But harmful touches, like hitting or kicking, are hurtful and threaten our safety.

Your voice influences your message: A good speaker uses their voice to express their emotions and maintain the listener's interest. An animated voice can report a visit to the dentist in an entertaining way, while a flat, dull tone can make an overseas holiday sound boring. Each voice is unique, and how you speak – whether low or high, fast or slow, soft or loud – influences how others perceive you. It's also important to know when to speak or listen, and a reasonable time to interrupt.

Check it out

- *"I did not say he hit my cat."* This sentence has eight words. Say it eight times and stress a different word each time. Does the meaning stay the same or does it change?

Some signs of verbal communication

Words: Non-verbal communication, like gestures, is important for connecting with others, but the words you use also matter. Words show who you are, what you think and how you feel. They bring people closer or push them apart. Just like fashion changes, language and swear words change over time, and different schools or cultures might use different words based on age or who they're talking to, like a peer or grandparent. Some students struggle with speech due to genetics or stress, but professional support is available.

Pronouns: Pronouns simplify conversations as they refer to people or things without constantly repeating their names. The right pronoun helps us communicate clearly, respectfully and assertively. Personal pronouns like 'I', 'you' and 'they' help us talk about ourselves, our listeners or about other people.

- **Using 'I':** When you start a sentence with 'I', you're expressing your own feelings, thoughts or experiences. For example, *"I feel upset when..."* or *"I think this is unfair."* This helps others understand how *you* feel without blaming them, avoids misunderstandings and keeps the conversation pleasant.

- **Using 'you':** When you start a sentence with 'you', it can sound like you're blaming or accusing someone, even if that's not what you meant. For example, *"You didn't tell me you were meeting somewhere else."* That's why it's better to use 'I' when you want to share your own thoughts or feelings.

- **Using 'they':** When you use 'they', you're making a general statement about a group of people or someone not present. For example, *"They always give us homework."* This is useful when talking about general things that happen to everyone, but it's less personal and precise than using 'I' or 'you'.

Family chat

- What's the difference when using 'I,' 'you' or 'they'? Give examples.

Your communication skills checklist

- Show a friendly smile, use comfortable eye contact and say hello.
- Listen carefully and show interest with your body, voice and words.
- Find five interesting questions to ask, for example, about school, sport, hobbies, family or apps.
- Chit-chat to build trust, for example, about the weather, snacks or social media.
- Find common topics of interest to create a connection.
- Interrupt when appropriate, but not constantly.
- When you feel safe and comfortable, share personal details about yourself.
- Check their reactions to avoid boring them.
- Find constructive statements to respectfully disagree, decline or challenge them.
- Decide whether to make arrangements, for example, *"Let's get together"* or move away.

Just do it

♦ Ask someone to video you or record yourself talking about your favourite chocolate or a holiday. When you watched the replay, did you appear friendly and interesting? If not, repeat until you're pleased.

Take action

♦ Find someone new to chat to and arrange to meet them again.

CHAPTER 7

Manage difficult, dodgy or dangerous people

Meerkats share a high level of social cohesion, empathy and cooperation. Their facial expressions are different when they playfight or fight seriously. They manage threats by working together and using different alarm calls. One acts as a lookout to warn the group, then, as a group, they puff up, hiss, lunge or retreat into their burrows.

If you're nice, then others will be nice to you

That's easy for adults to say! But it doesn't always work. Nobody's nice all the time. Besides, some kids don't care how you feel, due to their stress or peer pressure. So, being nice means being considerate to others while protecting yourself. If disputes occur, it's important to be respectful and cooperative but construct boundaries.

You need to know when and how to stand up for yourself or compromise. Use your mirror neurons to understand their perspective and calmly negotiate a reasonable solution. If not, agree to disagree. Thus, another social **superpower** involves finding ways to fix misunderstandings or handle tricky situations without attacking or retaliating. That improves relationships, builds respect and trust; if not, move away.

Confronting conflict

Balls don't always bounce the same way. Likewise, kids' feelings change from day to day. When you disagree with someone, it's important to know how to solve the problem while remaining friendly. When you share your feelings, it's better to say, for example, *"I felt left out when..."* instead of *"You never include me."* Then other students can understand your feelings without feeling blamed and defensive. If you ignore your feelings, you'll feel bad or have a tantrum, which makes everything worse. Besides, nobody's perfect, so you can't always be right. If you apologise for something minor, for example, saying, *"I'm sorry for interrupting you"* (which I'm sure you do), it may diffuse the dispute. Then, you can make up, leave or blend in.

Tips for dealing with disputes

- Ask questions – *"I don't understand why you're upset...?"*
- Explain – *"This is how I feel when you do this to me."*
- Provide a neutral statement – *"That's interesting"* or *"Thanks for telling me."*
- Ask for information – *"What's your evidence?"*
- Refuse a request – *"Sorry, not today."*
- Apologise – *"Sorry, I missed your point"* or *"Sorry, my ears were blocked."*

> ### Family chat
> - Share examples of how you resolved a conflict. Do you give in, fight back or negotiate? For example, with a sibling, parent or schoolmate.
> - What can your parents do when you're being emotional?
> - How does your family confront serious issues, or do they avoid them? Give examples.

What's bullying?

Many students who some classmates regard as being fat, dumb, rich or ugly are never bullied, while many talented, sporty, attractive and intelligent kids *are* bullied. The same goes for famous movie stars, entertainers, sportspeople and even royals like Princess Catherine, Princess of Wales, who was bullied at school in Year 7. Bullying is an abuse of power.

There are different kinds of bullying, like teasing, excluding, spreading malicious rumours, cyberbullying and physical bullying. One in three school students is bullied worldwide, despite many excellent but underutilised school-bullying programs. Sadly, most parents, schools and mental health professionals still don't understand the brain and body injuries caused by bullying.

> ### Pair and share
> - Have you ever been bullied?
> - What about your friends?
> - Did it affect either of you in any way?

Why is bullying bad?

While bantering among friends is fine, bullying is very harmful. Bullying makes you feel humiliated and ostracised; it means, *"You're no good, go away."* So, when someone teases you, for example, saying, *"You are fat, stupid, or gay"*, spreads malicious rumours, excludes you or steals your stuff, it's like casting a life-threatening, brain-altering spell over you. When you're told that *"You don't deserve to live"*, it's debilitating because humans survive better when they are respected and belong to social groups.

Whether the bullying is subtle or physical, it constitutes a social injury. Bullying damages your brain, injures your physical and emotional wellbeing, and alters your personality. It constitutes a social trauma that leaves permanent scars. It erodes your self-esteem, making it harder to play, socialise and feel included. It can affect your schoolwork, career choices and casual or close social relationships.

Bullying also harms the bully and their brain, damaging their future relationships, careers, health and self-esteem. Sadly, most bystanders won't support a target because they're scared of being bullied next. They know it's wrong and become upset while feeling powerless to stop it. Instinctively, some parents and teachers might feel powerless and experience some triggers or memories of their earlier bullying experiences.

Check it out

- Why does bullying affect everyone involved, including bystanders?
- Ask your parents if they were ever bullied and how it affected them.
- Why should you identify and block bullying behaviours early on, even if they seem minor?

Why do bullies bully?

Most bullies have emotional problems that they hide inside, even though they appear tough. When they bully others, they feel powerful by hiding their vulnerabilities, which rewards and encourages them to continue bullying. However, bullies bully because they get away with it at school or at home. But they also need a target who shows their distress, even if the bully says they were *"just joking"*. Unfortunately, many adults give false advice like *"Ignore the bullying"*, *"Do nothing"*, *"Walk away"* or *"Tell the bully to stop"*. This is impossible when you're upset and targets don't realise that their distress, which everyone knows, threatens the bully's survival instinct. Thus, they retaliate first to protect themselves. That's when I say, *"When you get upset or fight back, you make a bully happy."*

Check it out

♦ When something goes wrong, ask yourself, *"Why are they acting in a mean way to me? Did I do anything that might have affected the way they are reacting to me?"*

Manage difficult, dodgy or dangerous people

Types of bullying

Physical bullying: From pulling your hair, tearing your clothes, punching or kicking, there are many types of physical bullying. It includes stealing and damaging your possessions and making you feel physically unsafe. Make sure that you record this on your device and show it to your parents, school and the police.

Give it a go

♦ What can you do to stand up to physical bullying for yourself or someone else? For example, block the bully with safe martial arts, tickle them, video them, fart, cough, report it to your school or the police.

Teasing: The most common type of bullying is verbal, which makes you feel really embarrassed. This includes name-calling, insults, criticising your looks, intelligence, handicaps, sporting ability, family, religion, culture, gender, colourism or even your name.

Check it out

♦ Whether it happens once or many times, verbal teasing hurts and may be remembered forever. Why do you think teasing hurts for so long?

Pair and share

- Write down your five common teases. Practise different replies with someone you trust and use their feedback or video your replies to improve. Use good eye contact, keep a calm voice, stand up straight and disguise your stress. Act like a robot or avatar and block the teaser using a neutral style.

- You can handle teasing by agreeing, disagreeing, challenging, questioning, using humour or simply replying with something neutral like, *"And…?"*, *"That's interesting"*, *"Are you a reporter?"* or *"I'll ask AI tonight."*

Social exclusion: Social exclusion or ostracism occurs when you're kicked out of your group, either briefly or permanently, because you don't fit in and, therefore, threaten the others in the group. Ostracism is a fear tactic because nobody likes being rejected. It forces you to conform. Otherwise, you'll be excluded. This is extremely distressing, especially when former friends say things like, *"Go away"*, *"You don't belong"*, or *"Nobody wants you".* Although friendly gossip creates a social bond, malicious rumours and other gossip can be destructive and harmful. Always think carefully before you spread gossip.

Pair and share

- Tell a friend who has been mean to you how you feel about the way they've treated you and watch their feedback.
Do they care about hurting your feelings? If they don't, what can you do?

Give it a go

♦ Sometimes, a group excludes you because you appear different. You could try finding similar behaviours and common interests to behave more like them. Begin by reading the room to check out how others behave and then copy their style of relating.

Cyberbullying: Keyboard bullies use digital technology to embarrass, hurt or ruin other people. Cyberbullying takes place via computers, smartphones, social media and messaging apps. It can include sending nasty messages, texts or posts, sharing mean rumours or creating fake accounts. Cyberbullying can happen anytime, day or night, and can be witnessed by nearly everyone. In countries like Australia, cyberbullying is a crime.

Check it out

♦ How does cyberbullying differ from other types of bullying?

♦ What action can you take if you're being cyberbullied?

Family chat

♦ Do your parents check what you do online regularly? If not, why not?

How can you manage bullying?

Can you imagine playing tennis with a cricket bat or football with a golf ball? That's no longer cricket or football! Likewise, bullying is a game, and if you play by the bully's rules, they will win, and you will lose. Bullies want their targets to become upset, so stop doing that. Stay calm and neutral, then find constructive ways to manage or deflect the bully's game. If your tactics don't work after a week or so, get more effective strategies from your family, teachers, friends or school counsellor. Fortunately, there are many simple, safe and sensible ways to block bullies at school and later in life. See the tips below on dealing with bullies and check out the references at the end of this book.

Tips on blocking bullies

Remain calm: When a bully tries to make you feel awful but you remain calm, neutral and rational, their bullying boomerangs back on them. If you're lucky, they'll be surprised and shocked by your calm reaction. Their eyes may widen, their mouth may droop and they may shake their head in disbelief. This shows they've lost the power to hurt you and became embarrassed. Since nobody likes feeling embarrassed, they'll stop. But don't smile in front of them; save it for later when you tell your family.

Family chat

♦ When kids block a bully, other kids respect them, and some may become friends. Discuss with your family why this happens.

Become an active bystander: Being a social being involves confronting bullying behaviours, reporting them or comforting a hurt target. Supporting a bullied kid and chatting with them helps them feel less alone. Active witnesses report with their evidence. This validates the target and helps the bully become more responsible in future.

Dealing with abuse, violence and criminal behaviour

Sometimes, students cross a line from playing rough to becoming abusive. This can make you feel unsafe and scared, both physically and emotionally. Even if the bully has a traumatic history, that's no excuse for hurting others. From a young age, your gut instincts will tell you when something is wrong. When that happens, tell someone – your family, doctor, teacher, counsellor or the police. Don't keep it to yourself, because it will affect your health and wellbeing, and damage your trust in people. Getting help is the first step.

Family chat

♦ Discuss with your parents how to tell the difference between playful behaviour and something that crosses a safety line. Who could you feel safe telling if something bad happened?

CHAPTER 8

Everyone needs a social support system

Kangaroos socialise in groups called mobs. These mobs keep kangaroos safe from animals that want them for a snack. In each mob, there's a strong leader, usually a large male kangaroo, who protects everyone. They communicate by thumping their tails on the ground or making grunting and clicking sounds. This helps them work together as a big family.

Feeling connected helps people and animals thrive, but since the COVID-19 pandemic, many teens feel lonelier, replacing real friends with pets or screens. Screens have their place because texting and social media keep us in touch. However, face-to-face communication provides benefits that screens will never offer. When we're with others in person, we can read their expressions and body language, helping us feel more connected. Thus, balancing screen time with real-life social connections boosts your wellbeing, reduces stress and strengthens your feelings of support and social inclusion.

Your social life

Although most kids love ice cream, they need a variety of foods. Likewise, it's nice to have a bestie, but sometimes they move away. You only need a small group of classmates, not the whole class. It's also nice to make a variety of friends from different social groups, as they spice up your social life. Our social connections range from casual ones, like having a brief chat, and informal ones, like talking with classmates, to good friendships that grow when you spend real time together. Close relationships involve trusting your friends, while intimate relationships are the closest, where you share everything with those who are very special to you.

You'll find that some friendships are low maintenance, while others are high maintenance. If your friendship rate isn't reciprocal, then rearrange it to protect yourself. Whether you're at school, playing sports or just hanging out, find friends your age, younger or older, but don't allow anyone to bully you. Regardless of whether friendships are brief or last for years, each one helps you grow and learn more about yourself and others. Making these friendships work is another social **superpower**.

Check it out

♦ What can you do to increase your social connections?

What are your social smarts?

This is not a trick question! This book gives you many strategies for becoming a more friendly, sociable person. Although you may be different to others – because everyone is unique, just like a patchwork doll – when you practise these social skills regularly, they'll help you gather a variety of friends and social groups.

The average social kid:

- Is friendly, respectful, compassionate
- Uses good non-verbal and verbal communication skills
- Absorbs feedback from their friends
- Knows when to follow or challenge the group
- Belongs to several groups because no single group can fulfil all their social needs
- Knows when to install boundaries when they're being mistreated
- Expects good friends to help out and reduce some of their stress and loneliness

Being socially smart means making friends without the drama and handling weird stuff like a pro. You stay cool, bounce back fast, and avoid feeling like a lonely potato at school and in life.

The social smarts formula

Here are some strategies you can adopt to help you become a more friendly, sociable person:

1. Be friendly

When you're with other kids, become relaxed and friendly. Make eye contact, smile and talk about fun, simple things. Ask questions about what they like – this helps you connect and avoids awkward silences. Listening and giving friendly responses keeps the conversation going. If they want to chat, they'll stay; if not, they'll move away. Remember, how you act, like being kind and approachable, matters more than the words you use.

> ### Just do it
> ♦ What are five basic questions you can use for girls or boys?

2. Shift your focus

It's normal to feel nervous about getting along with others, but focusing too much on your own fears makes it even harder to connect. Imagine walking on a narrow bridge; if you look down, you might lose your balance, but you can be focused if you look ahead. The same goes for making friends. When you focus on the other person and show genuine interest with relevant questions, it's easier to connect and build stronger friendships.

> **Check it out**
> - Why do you think that focusing on others, instead of yourself, gives you the confidence to chat more freely?

3. Show empathy

Empathy means understanding how someone else feels, like being happy for a dog when it gets a bone, even though you wouldn't want it. You can't know exactly what someone else feels, but you can imagine what they're experiencing. Kids like people who like them, and a kind, caring kid makes an attractive friend. While being *nice* is a habit to please others or stay safe, being *kind and caring* is a valuable social survival skill. When you show empathy, you needn't worry about what others think of you, because most students respect a caring person. This is another social **superpower**.

Take action

- You could become an everyday hero who does kind, brave or helpful things for others, without seeking credit, regardless of any difficult experiences you have had in the past or are having now.

- Check out *The Hero's Journey* by Joseph Campbell. Can you find similar stories in books and films? Why don't you write a story about your life as an everyday hero in training?

Family chat

- Discuss why showing empathy helps you build better relationships.

4. Be yourself

It's hard for most teens to be true to themselves because they're changing all the time. But it's even harder when you try to act the way you *think* others want you to – especially when you're only guessing what they expect. You might guess wrong! People can usually tell when you're not being real, and that makes it harder to speak up, show confidence and earn their respect. When you become more genuine about your current life, others will find it easier to trust you. Being yourself helps you build real friendships and feel more comfortable with who you are.

Let it go

- How can sharing a small slice of your worries improve your friendships?
- Try being just a little more 'you' this week – whether it's answering a question honestly in class, sharing your opinion in a group or telling a friend something true and even painful about yourself. You might be surprised who connects with the real you.

5. Negotiate

It's normal to have different opinions. Sometimes, you'll agree, other times, you will disagree or compromise. But make sure your friends listen and respect your ideas and vice versa. Avoid friends who try to ignore, manipulate, control or belittle you.

Family chat

♦ How can sharing different opinions build better friendships?

6. Commitment

Real friends are loyal and respect your feelings most of the time. They become active bystanders when others are mean and support you when things go wrong. If you upset them, they can usually forgive you and move on. But don't take advantage of that; if they can't respect your feelings, it's time to find better friends.

Pair and share

♦ When you use the word 'I', how will the feedback show that your friend respects your feelings or not?

7. Do it now

Popular kids plan their social lives by constantly making arrangements. If you want to have a better social life, then you need to take the initiative by chatting with classmates, suggesting plans and inviting others to join. Don't wait for other shy kids to contact you, spend lunchtime in the library or be alone. Don't get upset waiting for others to make the first move – take the initiative and start connecting.

Take action

♦ What are steps you can take towards making new friends?

8. Feedback

Tiffany didn't like artificial deodorants, but classmates resented her body odour and spread rumours. When her teacher recommended a natural deodorant, the gossip stopped.

Everywhere you go, you receive different kinds of feedback. Positive feedback boosts your confidence; negative feedback damages your self-esteem; constructive feedback helps you improve, communicate better and build your self-respect. Sportspeople and entertainers rely on feedback to improve. So, when someone smiles, compliments you or invites you to play, grab it as a self-esteem booster. If the feedback is helpful, learn from it, if it's not useful, let it go. Feedback is another social **superpower**.

Family chat

♦ Can you think of five to 10 games that rely on feedback from others?

♦ How does different types of feedback – positive, negative and constructive – help you improve your friendships?

9. Nobody's perfect

Everyone is different. Some kids like plain chips, others like them flavoured. You won't please everyone, and that's OK. No one's perfect – not you, your friends or your family. People make mistakes or might act mean sometimes, but that doesn't mean you should get even.

Some kids only talk about themselves or dominate a conversation, while others expect everyone to play by their rules. Some appear arrogant but may be shy or neurodiverse. Of course, some kids don't like you because they're jealous or intimidated by your achievements or you're not reading them correctly. If they exclude you, don't worry, just remain neutral and pleasant, and find better friends.

Pair and share

- Find a classmate. Each person shares something unkind they've said recently – at school, at home or with a friend.
- On your turn, discuss why you did that. Then share how you want others to treat you when you mess up.
- Discuss what kind of person you want to be, even when people are being mean.

10. Enjoy being with your friends

It's important to have friends who make you feel good and with whom you enjoy being with. Playing and having fun isn't just about enjoying yourself – it helps you build important skills like thinking creatively, solving problems, reducing stress and collaborating with others. Enjoying their company and giving back to others releases chemicals in your brain that lower stress and make you feel happier, which helps you connect better, strengthen friendships and achieve more function.

Family chat

♦ What do you think are the most important skills you learn from spending time with friends?

Your social smarts checklist

Find out how confident and socially smart you are becoming by seeing how you perform in the table below.

What social skills do you use and how often?	Never	Sometimes	Often
• I use the phone/internet for a chat (with real friends)			
• I use the phone/social media to make arrangements			
• I approach kids I don't know to play every week			
• I use the phone/internet to do homework with others			
• I socialise with the same friends nearly every day			
• I always mention the same friends or bullies at the dinner table			
• I show concern for unhappy classmates			
• I invite friends my age for games, movies or sleepovers			
• I participate in sports or other activities with peers			
• I receive and give birthday party invitations			
• I make or buy gifts for friends, compliment them and share nice activities			

Conclusion

During a recent Australian bushfire, koalas who were starved of their special gum leaves were so thirsty that they approached people and drank water from their hands and bottles!

There are many stories about terrified animals who learn how to trust a human being for sustenance, shelter and affection. Many adults are shy inside, but over time, they build successful social and work relationships. I'm one of them! This is the book I wish I could have read in my old school library when I began secondary school, because I was bullied and became shy. For many years, I couldn't understand how some kids created and enjoyed a normal social life.

Some readers may have lost confidence making friends, due to COVID-19 or other stressors. But waiting to find confidence is like digging for gold. Many behaviours seem hard at first, like hitting a ball or tying shoelaces, but become easy with practice. Likewise, good social skills don't suddenly appear like magic – they involve hard work and practice. Most animals aren't born with their social survival skills, they need to learn them from their families. Everyone makes mistakes, and if you just keep doing the same thing, you'll get the same results. The secret is to take small steps, improve your social skills, get feedback, change your behaviours and practice. Then repeat this again. When you're a nice, caring person, you make it easier for kids to like you.

Let's review the social superpowers in this book:

1. Use your facial muscles – to show interest and friendliness, when appropriate.
2. Develop your mirror neurons – they allow you to connect with others by empathising.

3. Increase your understanding – of someone's feelings, actions and lived experiences to become more mindful.
4. Improve your self-esteem to empower you to connect constructively and assertively with others.
5. Accept yourself as you are right now – this allows others to respect you and like being with you.
6. Be cheerful – it is more attractive than being a worrywart.
7. Show empathy – this helps others value you as a caring person.
8. Accept feedback – constructive feedback helps you learn while positive feedback boosts your self-esteem.
9. Make social arrangements – this allows some of your friendships to flourish.
10. Avoid attacking back – find better ways to fix misunderstandings or handle tricky situations.

Try to use these social superpowers every day.

Pair and share

- Discuss how many superpowers you found in this book.
- Have you found another superpower that I've missed? Write them down.

Although life is never perfect and everyone has joyful and stressful times, when you have family, friends and others who support, advise and guide you, and with whom you can experience special moments of social connection, then the ups and downs of life are far easier to manage.

Living life as a social being is the best way to be happier, healthier and achieve more of your life's goals. I hope that this book can give you many simple, social tips to enjoy your life.

Evelyn M. Field OAM

References

Blakemore, S.J., & Mills, K.L. (2014). Is adolescence a sensitive period for sociocultural processing? *Annual Review of Psychology, 65*, 187–207.

Campbell, J. (2014). *The Hero's Journey*. New World Library.

Dunbar, R.I.M. (2009). The social brain hypothesis and its implications for social evolution. *Annals of Human Biology, 36*(5), 562–572.

Field, E.M. (2023). *Bully Blocking: Empowering students to deflect and protect themselves from bullying*. Amba Press.

Lieberman, M.D. (2013). *Social: Why Our Brains Are Wired to Connect*. Crown Publishers.

Lim, M.H., Eres R., & Vasan S. (2020). Understanding loneliness in the twenty-first century: an update on correlates, risk factors, and potential solutions. *Social Psychiatry and Psychiatric Epidemiology, 55*(7), 793–810.

Siebert, C. (2016). What Does a Parrot Know About PTSD? *The New York Times Magazine*.

Sparks, S.D. (2023). What Educators Need to Know About the 'Epidemic of Loneliness' Among Students. *Education Week*.

UNICEF. (2021). *The State of the World's Children 2021 – On My Mind: Promoting, protecting and caring for children's mental health*. New York.

www.ingramcontent.com/pod-product-compliance
Lightning Source LLC
Chambersburg PA
CBHW052114070526
44584CB00017B/2472